Sports

A letter from the Author

Hello!

*Welcome to **Sports**!*
People play and watch sport all over the world. It's a good international link – a way to find friends in other countries. We explore the international face of sport here.

There are also lots of interesting facts about sport. Why does the Marathon have that name? Why do we have the Olympic Games every four years? Why do people play cricket in some countries?

We also look at the positive and negative parts of sport. Is it always good for everybody? Of course, there is one other big question. What is a "sport"? How is it different from "activity"? Is dancing a sport? Or playing chess? Is all sport competitive? Well, the dictionary says that a sport is an activity with rules, or a code of practice. What do you think?

Lots of questions! The Sports Detective spot asks a few more. Use your personal ideas, your experience and your interests. Become a sports expert. Good luck!

Susan Holden

contents

TO THE **TOPICS** USERS

VOCABULARY You can find the key vocabulary for every article in the **WORD FILE** on that page. The pictures will also help you to guess the meaning in context. There is a summary of useful vocabulary on the **Check it out** page. Finally, you can use the *Macmillan Essential Dictionary* to consolidate the new vocabulary.

WEBSITES There is a list of useful website addresses on page 2. Remember that websites change. Be selective!

Check it out

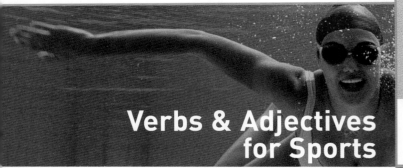

Verbs & Adjectives for Sports

| goal | gold/silver/bronze medal |
| point | rule | score |

Watching

celebrate   cheer   support

Playing

beat	compete	hit
lose	practice 🇺🇸	practise 🇬🇧
score	train	win

Describing (adjectives)

| boring | dangerous | disappointing |
| exciting | fast | slow |

Soccer/Football

coach	field 🇺🇸	forward
goal	manager	midfielder
pitch 🇬🇧	player	referee

Events

| championship | competition | event |
| game | match | race |

Tennis

court	deuce (40-40)	game
love (zero points)	net	point
racket	set	umpire

People

athlete	captain	club
coach	commentator	competitor
fan	personal trainer	player
runner	spectator	team

Sources and Resources

We consulted a lot of sources for 'Sports': people, books and the Internet. If you want to find out more about any of the topics, here are some useful Internet sites. Add your own favourite sites and other useful resources.

Olympic games: www.museum.olympic.org
City marathons: www.wikipedia.org
       www.ingnycmarathon.org
Sport and charity ("Save the Rhino" and rhino facts): www.savetherhino.org
Different sports: www.bbc.co.uk/cbbc/sport
Judo: www.judoinfo.com
Polo: www.polo.co.uk
Sports and fair trade: www.maketradefair.com
Famous football stars: www.wsoccer.com/players

Places

stadium   tennis court   track

Sport:
to do or to watch?

Some people play a sport. Others prefer to watch it. What are their reasons? (Read more opinions on page 12.)

Way of Life

I live near the sea, so swimming is part of my life! I meet my friends on the beach, and we have fun. There are exciting sports, like surfing, too.
A.J., 19, Australia

Excitement

Soccer's my favourite sport. It's really exciting. It's good to play and it's good to watch. I always want my team to win. In fact, I identify with my team. When they win, I'm really happy. But when they lose, I'm in a bad mood all day!
T.Y., 17, Japan

Travel

Sports people travel a lot. Players go to other cities to compete. Sometimes they go to other countries. Today, spectators travel, too. There are matches and competitions everywhere. Some people take their holidays to watch sport: the World Cup, the Olympics. Sport is international!
M.O., 18, Brazil

Health

I play tennis. You feel great. You run and jump, and you're in the fresh air. I always want to win! I watch tennis on T.V., too. It's exciting. I love the Wimbledon championships. Every year, I have a favourite player. It's a good game for men and women.
P.H., 15, Argentina

New Skills

It's exciting to learn a new skill. At first, you can't do something and then, one day, you can do it! Success is good for people. It makes them feel self-confident.
J.L., 14, Mexico

WORD FILE

addict	A person who likes a particular activity very much.
championship	A competition to determine a champion.
compete (v)	To be part of a competition.
dream about (v)	To think about things that can be possible.
feel (v)	To have a specific emotion.
fresh air	The air outdoors.
health	The condition of your body.
lose (v)	To not win a competition.
match	A sports competition.
mood	The way people feel (happy, sad, angry etc.).
self-confident	Feeling that you can do things well.
skill	The ability to do something well.
spectator	A person who watches a sport.
success	Doing something well.
way of life	What people do every day.
win (v)	To be first in a competition.

🇺🇸		🇬🇧
favorite		favourite
ocean		sea
vacations		holidays

TV Addict

I love to watch sport – on T.V.! It's all there – skiing, hang gliding, horse jumping, and lots more. I can't see these things in my town, but I can watch them at home. I can dream and perhaps, one day...!
L.M., 20, USA

Do you do any sports? If not, why not? If yes – what sports do you do? What sports do you watch? What sports do you dream about?

Check the reports of the 2004 Athens Olympics. Make

GRΣΣCΣ

THE ANCIENT OLYMPICS

The Olympic Games begin in Ancient Greece. The first written record: 776 B.C. The last Ancient Games: 393 A.D. That's more than 1,000 years!

Olympus is a special town for the Games. Sport and religion are important for the Ancient Greeks. The event is in honour of the god Zeus. There is a temple in Olympus, and a big stadium – 20,000 spectators can watch the Games. All the athletes are men, and all the spectators are men, too.

The competitors do not wear any clothes. The competitions are races (400 metres and 5,000 metres), chariot-racing, boxing, and the pentathlon (running, long jump, discus, javelin and wrestling). You can see pictures of these sports on Ancient Greek pots.

During these Games, every four years, all wars stop. The cities of Ancient Greece are at peace.

THE MODERN OLYMPICS

Athens 1896

At the end of the 19th century, a Frenchman, Philippe de Coubertin, wants to revive the Olympic Games. In 1896, he organises the first modern Games in Athens. There are 295 athletes from 13 countries, and 40,000 spectators. After this, there are Games every four years. But when there is a war (1914-18 and 1939-45), there are no Games.

WORD FILE	
ancient	Very old.
athlete	A person who takes part in a sports competition.
in honour of	To show respect to a person.
javelin	A long pointed stick to throw in sports competition.
peace	The opposite of war.
represent (v)	To use a symbol for a person or event.
revive (v)	To make something happen again.
ring	A circle.
spectator	A person who watches a sport.
stadium	A large building for sports events.
value	An important personal belief.
war	Conflict between states or nations.
wrestling	A sport in which a person holds and throws the other person.

honor	honour
meter	metre
organize (v)	organise (v)

Athens 2004

The five Olympic rings are in Athens again! Each ring represents a different continent. For the Greeks, this is an important moment. The modern world remembers the values of the Ancient World.

ATHENS 2004

SPECIAL OLYMPICS

The Paralympics

Every four years, disabled people have their Games, too. Some of the sports in these Paralympics are the same as the events in the Olympics, but with different rules. Some of the sports are different. Here are a few examples:

Basketball and tennis: they play these sports in wheelchairs.

Goal-ball: a special game for blind players. There is a bell in the ball, so they can hear it.

Judo: blind people compete in this.

These Games are very popular. The competitors are very good and the events are exciting. Every year, there are new records and new champions. They win gold, silver and bronze medals, just like in the Olympic Games. Disabled people are good sports people too.

WORD FILE

bell	A metal object that makes a ringing sound.
blind	Not able to see.
bronze	A brown metal. Bronze medals are for 3rd place in a competition.
champion	The winner of an important competition.
competitor	A person who participates in a competition.
disabled	Unable to use part of your body.
event	An organised game or competition.
gold	A yellow metal. Gold medals are for 1st place in a competition.
medal	A round piece of metal for the winners of a competition.
record	The best result in a competition.
rule	Regulation.
silver	A white metal. Silver medals are for 2nd place in a competition.
wheelchair	A chair with wheels for people who cannot walk.
win (v)	To be first in a competition.

🇺🇸 favorite organized   🇬🇧 favourite organised

Winter Olympics

Skiing, skating, sledge races… these competitions take place every four years too. In the mountains, in the snow, the Winter Olympics have a special atmosphere.

Check if your favourite sport is in the Olympics. Who are the champions? What is the record?

SPORTS DETECTIVE

Marathon and

Νικη

Marathon: the place

The year: 490 B.C.

The place: Marathon and Athens, Greece.

The context: War between Persia and Athens.

The story: The Persians want to attack Athens. They land near Marathon. The Persian army is huge: 25,000 soldiers. There are 10,000 soldiers in the Athenian army. One of these, Pheidippides, is a famous runner. He runs 240 kilometres to Sparta, to ask for help. It is the middle of a big festival in Sparta, and the answer is "No, we can't help you!".

Pheidippides runs back (240 kilometres again) with the bad news. However, the Athenians win the battle. Athens is safe! And so Pheidippides runs to the city with the good news. The distance is only about 42 kilometres, but it is uphill. He arrives, says "Nike!" (victory) – and falls down, dead.

The new Marathon

The year: 1896.

The place: Marathon and Athens, Greece.

The context: The first modern Olympic Games.

The length: 42 kilometres.

The story: Greece are the hosts. Up to now, they have no medals. The marathon is the final event. Twenty-five runners begin the race on the bridge at Marathon. After 40 kilometres, a runner enters the stadium in Athens. The spectators give a huge cheer. The winner is a Greek postal worker, Spiridon Louis, from a small village. His time is 2 hours, 58 minutes, 50 seconds. Greece wins a gold medal!

WORD FILE

battle	A fight between two armies in a war.
cheer	A loud vocal noise to encourage the players.
host	A nation that arranges a special event and provides the area.
land (v)	To arrive at a place by plane or boat.
medal	A round piece of metal for the winners of a competition.
runner	A person who runs.
spectator	A person who watches a sport.
uphill	In the direction of the top of a hill.
war	Conflict between states or nations.

 kilometer   kilometre

The New York Marathon

The year: 1970-now.

The place: New York.

The context: The first big city race.

The story: In 1976, only 55 runners finish – and no women! Now around 40,000 people take part. From 1970-75, the race is in Central Park, but now the runners go through the streets of the five districts of New York: Staten Island, Brooklyn, Queens, the Bronx and Manhattan.

Marathons

A hot Marathon

Event: The Marathon des Sables.
Place: The Sahara Desert, North Africa.
Length: 226 kilometres.
Problems: Temperatures of 49°C.

Running is for young people: true or false?

False! Fauja Singh is 93 years old in 2004! He is a Sikh, and he competes in the London Marathon. His time in 2003: 6 hours, 2 minutes and 43 seconds. He really wants to do it in less than 6 hours!

Fauja Singh raises money for charities. He's a vegetarian, and he doesn't smoke or drink alcohol. He meditates every morning, and he trains every day in the streets near his son's house.

Animals too!

Today, every marathon helps raise money for charity. Cancer, heart disease, educational projects, poor people – running can help all these. Marathons even help animals!

"Save the Rhino" is a charity. Its marathon runners wear rhino costumes in the marathons in New York, London, Los Angeles, Boston, Paris and Durban. Why? The Sumatran Rhino is in danger – there are only 300 animals in the world (and four of them in zoos).

WORD FILE

charity	An organisation to help people in difficulties.
costume	Clothes with a particular appearance.
meditate (v)	To think about one thing.
raise money (v)	To collect money.
train (v)	To practise for a sports competition.
vegetarian	A person who does not eat meat.

🇺🇸 kilometer	🇬🇧 kilometre
practice (v)	practise (v)

7

THE A-Z OF SPORT

A

BASEBALL
<u>Easy description</u>: You hit a hard ball with a big bat. You run round four places (bases). The other team (fielders) try to get the ball to the bases before you arrive.

<u>Training</u>: Run fast, throw the ball.

How many different sports are there in the world? Any ideas? Of course, many of these are international, so it's easy to think of these – soccer, tennis, swimming. Some of them are national – sports like sumo wrestling (Japan), or *capoeira* (Brazil). Other sports, like skateboarding, or water gymnastics are popular with a specific group of people. Perhaps only a small number of people play or watch them.

Some sports begin in one country, and then travel to a different one. You can read more about these on page 13. We don't know the total number of sports, but how about an *alphabet* of sports? Well, there are 26 letters in the English alphabet, aren't there? Unfortunately, we don't have space for 26 sports – but here are descriptions of a few. We ask two questions: "What happens?" and "How can you improve or win?"

WHAT?   Our basic description of the sport.
HOW?   Things to practise.

C

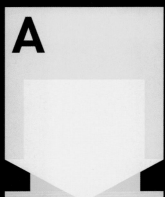

DIVING
<u>Easy description</u>: You dive into the water.
BUT: You win points with clever movements AND some of the dives are 10 metres high!

<u>Training</u>: Practise entering the water with no splashes.

WORD FILE

backwards	In the direction behind you.
bat	A long piece of wood to hit a ball.
dive into (v)	To jump into water especially headfirst.
improve (v)	To make something better.
practise (v)	To get ready for a sports event.
safety gear	Clothes or equipment to protect your body.
skill	The ability to do something well.
speed	How quickly something moves.
spin (v)	To make a ball turn round.
splash	The sound of something falling into water.
strength	Feeling strong.
throw (v)	To send something through the air with your hand.
trick	A clever action.

meter	metre
ocean	sea
pants	trousers
practice (v)	practise (v)
soccer	football

E

G

H

FIGURE-SKATING
<u>Easy description</u>: You dance on the ice – to music.
<u>Training</u>: Don't fall over. Practise stopping suddenly.

Q

POLO
<u>Easy description</u>: Two teams
on small, fast horses (ponies)
try to hit a ball into the goals
<u>Training</u>: Find a fast pony!

ATEBOARDING
y description: You do
ks on a skateboard.
d tricks win points.
ning: Practise jumping.
ar safety gear.

RUNNING
<u>Easy description</u>: You run a
distance, very fast. It can be
short (100 metres) or long
(a marathon).
<u>Training</u>: Run every day.
Check your time.

Z

O

BLE TENNIS
y description: You hit
nall ball over a net on
ble.
ning: Practise spinning
ball.

U

Y

NETBALL
<u>Easy description</u>: You try to
put the ball into your
opponent's net. You can't run
or hold the ball for more
than three seconds.
It's very fast!
<u>Training</u>: Practise throwing
the ball into an empty
container.

LEYBALL
y description: Players
ball over a high net
their hands.
ning: Like table tennis –
the ball a spin.

WINDSURFING
<u>Easy description</u>: You ride
on a board with a big sail.
You do it on the sea or a
big lake.
<u>Training</u>: Practise fast turns.

X

M

HOCKEY
description: Two
s play on ice with sticks.
hit a hard piece of
er (puck) into the goals.
ning: Practise skating
wards. Wear lots of
es.

JUDO
<u>Easy description</u>: You try to
throw your opponent. You
win points for a good throw.
<u>Training</u>: Put your judo belt
in your trousers, like a tail.
Try to pull out everybody's tail.

K

LONG JUMP
<u>Easy description</u>: You try to
jump as far as possible.
<u>Training</u>: Jump as near the
mark as possible.

THE PRICE OF $PORT

Sports fans buy soccer shirts for their favourite teams. They collect autographs from their favourite players, too. Trainers, sports caps and tracksuits are part of fashion today. People want the "in" labels and designs. They also want cheap prices.

Sports clothes are big business too! When there's a big sport event, like the World Cup, or the Olympic Games, the big sportswear companies want to sell clothes with the "magic" logo.

Where do these things come from? Who makes them? It's not always a happy story.

Workers in Asia make many of these things. Look at the labels. Many of them come from Indonesia, China, Cambodia and Thailand. And in some factories, people work long hours and receive low pay. Here is an example from a report in 2004. This report is from Oxfam, an international charity.

> I have many health problems: headaches, stomach flu, back pains…
> My target is 120 pairs of trousers in an hour.
> In the normal working day I make 960 pairs!
> We work from 8 a.m., … and we work until 2 a.m. or 3 a.m. in the peak season.

Some companies now have rules to protect their workers. And there's a new report from Oxfam, "Play Fair at the Olympics". It wants the IOC (International Olympics Committee) to help them.

WORD FILE

big business	Commercial activities that are very profitable.
charity	An organisation to help people in difficulties.
factory	A place where people make things.
label	A brand name of fashion designer.
peak season	The most important months.
protect (v)	To look after somebody.
rule	Regulation.
sports fan	A person who loves to watch sports.
sportswear	Clothes to play (or watch) sports.
target	The number of objects to make in a day.

🇺🇸 favorite	🇬🇧 favourite
pants	trousers
sweatshirt/sweatpants	tracksuit
sneakers	trainers

The Beautiful Game

Football (or soccer) is a really international game. Not just because national teams play against teams from other countries in international competitions like the World Cup, the Copa Americana or the Asia Cup.
Players can also play for clubs in different countries.

Here are some true international players. They play for a foreign club, and they also play in their national teams.

AHN JUNG-HWAN
Nationality:	Korean
Club Team:	FC Metz (Japan)
National Team:	Korea
Position:	Forward
Born:	27 January 1976

EXTRA FACT: The top player of Asia had a bad time in Italy.

RONALDO (THE PHENOMENON)
Nationality:	Brazilian
Club Team:	Real Madrid (Spain)
National Team:	Brazil
Position:	Forward
Born:	22 September 1976

EXTRA FACT: World Footballer of the year in 1996 and 1997.

DAVID BECKHAM
Nationality:	English
Club Team:	Real Madrid (Spain)
Position:	Midfielder
National Team:	England
Born:	02 May 1975

EXTRA FACT: Ambition (after football): To organise soccer schools for kids in different countries.

THIERRY HENRY
Nationality:	French (Guadeloupe)
Club Team:	Arsenal (England)
National Team:	France
Position:	Forward
Born:	17 August 1977

EXTRA FACT: He is a great attacker.

WORD FILE

forward (soccer) An attacking player.
midfielder (soccer) A player in the middle of the pitch.

🇺🇸 favorite	🇬🇧 favourite
field	pitch
organize	organise
soccer	football

Add new facts about these players. Then collect similar info about *your* favourite international football star.

SPORTS DETECTIVE

The two sides of sport

There are some positive reasons for doing sport on page 3.
Here are some more positive ideas, serious and not-so-serious:

POSITIVE

Social effects

Sport can help people in poor parts of the city. Doing sport can help them to fight against drugs and crime.

Lifeskills

There are winners and losers in sport. And there are winners and losers in life, too. So sport can prepare people for life. It can help us to overcome problems, and to help other people.

Fashion

Many sports clothes are great fashion. So doing sport can be a reason for looking good!

Fun

Sport gives lots of opportunities to have fun.

WORD FILE	
cheer (v)	To make a loud noise to encourage your team.
crime	A very bad action, against the law.
fan	A person who supports a sports team.
loser	The opposite of winner in a competition.
opportunity	A chance to do something.
overcome (v)	To succeed when there is a problem.
prepare (v)	To get ready for something.
train (v)	To practise a sport.
war	Conflict between states or nations.
winner	The victorious person in a competition.

🇺🇸 practice 🇬🇧 practise
    soccer   football

NEGATIVE

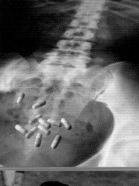

Think of your own "Two sides of sport".

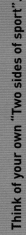

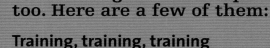

It's not all good news! Sport has its problems, too. Here are a few of them:

Training, training, training

Good athletes train every day. They often have no time for friends or fun. They forget about a "normal" life. After years of this, some of them say "No more!". Many tennis stars begin when they are 4 or 5 years old, and stop before they are 20.

Drugs

Athletes want to win. They eat special diets to be strong. Their bodies are very important for them. And sometimes they want to "help" their bodies. Drugs *can* do this – but then the competition isn't fair.

Sports people do tests of their blood and urine to detect drugs. Good players don't want to cheat.

Isolation

Sport is great if you like it. If all your friends are good at sport, and you are not, it's no fun. Sport at school can be horrible for some people.

Violence

It's natural to support a football team. It's normal to want your team to win. It's good to be excited, and to cheer a goal. And it's great to celebrate after the match.

But some fans make a lot of trouble. They fight other fans. They drink a lot of alcohol, and are violent. The police have to control them. It's not sport, it's war. And that's sad for the players, and sad for the other spectators.

Sport: import export

A lot of sports are international, we know. People play them in a lot of different countries. Why? How? What's the reason?

Well, some sports begin in one place, and then travel to different countries or regions. Some of them become international. Why do they travel? Who takes them? Let's take a look at a few.

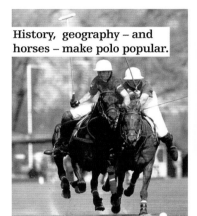

History, geography – and horses – make polo popular.

History can explain the development of a sport.

CRICKET

A hundred years ago, different parts of the world were part of the British Empire. The English have a favourite game: cricket. They play it in India, the West Indies, Australia and New Zealand. Now teams from these countries (and Pakistan and Sri Lanka) often beat the English teams. Cricket matches are very long. They can continue for five days!

POLO

Polo comes from Ancient China, Persia and India. It's very fast, exciting – and dangerous. In the 19th century, English soldiers take it from India to England. It becomes very popular and fashionable. Then it goes to the U.S., Ireland and Australia. English and Irish engineers and farmers take it to Argentina. The Argentinians have fast horses, so it becomes very popular here, too. Today, many of the champion players (and ponies) are Argentinian. It's still fast, it's still dangerous – and it's still very exciting to play and to watch.

JUDO

Judo comes from Ancient China and Japan. Sports like judo, kendo and aikido develop the body and the brain. It is not necessary to be big and strong to win.

Different cultures often like judo too.

Intelligence is important, too. Children can practise them. Now they are popular all over the world. Judo is a sport in the Olympic Games. Its rules continue to change and develop. It is an ancient sport with a modern face.

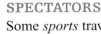

Travel developments affect sport.

SPECTATORS

Some *sports* travel, and today *people* travel, too. They go to see their football team play in a different town. When there's a big event, like the World Cup, many people save money and take their holiday. They travel to different countries to support their teams, or to see new ones. So sport can introduce them to new places, new experiences and new people. Of course, you can see these events on T.V., too – but real travel is better!

WORD FILE

beat (v)	To do something better than other people.
champion (player)	The best.
pony	A small horse.
popular	Lots of people like it.
rule	A regulation.

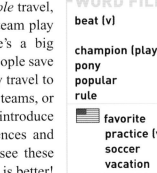 favorite
practice (v)
soccer
vacation

 favourite
practise (v)
football
holiday

13

Do you know?

(Answers on page 16.)

1. PUZZLE PIX

Match the sport.

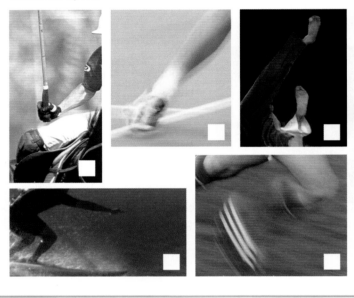

a baseball

b skateboarding

c football

d tennis

e surf

f polo

g judo

h skiing

2. SPORTS FACTS

Can you guess the sport? Sometimes there are two possibilities.

judo

cricket

tennis/table tennis

The marathon

a Snow, a mountain, and two pieces of wood. ●●●●
b Two or four players hit a ball over a net. ●●●●
c Can you run 42.2 kilometres? ●●●●
d Good players have black belts. ●●●●
e A match can go on for five days! ●●●●
f Argentinian horses help to win prizes. ●●●●
g Fat men are good at this. ●●●●
h Kids make magic on a piece of wood! ●●●●

skiing

polo

sumo wrestling

skateboarding

3. SPORTS EQUIPMENT

Connect the equipment to the sport.

10

9

2

3

☐ baseball
☐ cricket
☐ cycling
☐ hockey
☐ ice-skating
☐ rugby
☐ skateboarding
☐ table tennis
☐ tennis
☐ underwater swimming

8

7

6

4

5

Projects

Olympic Games

1

Collect facts about the last Olympic Games. Choose your favourite sport or sports. Work with some friends and make a wall-chart of photos, texts and medals.

Sport Blog

2

Write a blog about your sport activities. How do you train? What do you eat? What do you win or lose? What about watching sport? Are the results good or bad? How do you feel?

Sport Souvenirs

3

Design some souvenirs for your favourite sport.

Sport Diet

4

Choose a sport and work out a good diet for it.

Unusual Sports

5

Football, tennis, swimming – everyone knows about these sports! What about an unusual one? Or a crazy sport? Find the facts, or make up the rules. Present them with text and/or pictures.

Sports Survey

6

Do a sports survey in your class. Who plays sport? Who watches sport? What do they play or watch? Design a questionnaire. Decide a good way to present the results.

Sports Fashion Designer

7

Design some great sports clothes.

Sports Results

8

Choose a team or a sport competitor. Follow their progress for a month. Present the results.

Sports Stars

9

Choose a sports star and find out about him or her: e.g. personal life, favourite films or music.

The A-Z of Sport

10

Use the A-Z of sport on pages 8 and 9 to design your own sport board game. Draw it on a big piece of card. Make up some rules. Play the game in a group.

15

Fun Chat: Olympic Games

Hi, there! Are you an Olympics expert? Take a look at these two sports. They're really unusual – but they're both in the Summer Olympic Games. True!

Synchronized diving:
two people dive together.

Taekwondo:
you kick your opponent!

And the future? What about skateboarding? Or surfing? Or even rock climbing? Well, they're all recognised Olympic sports. Perhaps in 2012!

BTW   Can you match these places and dates? (Answers in the Facts Check – don't cheat!)

2006	Beijing
2008	Torino
2010	Vancouver

Which ones are Winter Games? Which one is Summer Games?

Note: BTW = "By the way" in webchat.

Teens Chat

Sarah: Hi. Do you like sports?

Lesley: Well… I go to the gym sometimes. What about you?

Sarah: Me too. And I'm into American football. I like to watch it. But there isn't a team at school. They play ordinary football, of course.

Lesley: What other sports?

Sarah: Oh – swimming. Athletics. Golf… But I'm not a sporty person!

Lesley: I'm not, either. All my family loves to do sports, but not me.

Can you believe it?

What's this?	A tree.
Who's this man?	A competitor.
What's he doing?	He's throwing a tree!
Where?	In Scotland.
Why?	It's a popular competition.
What's its name?	"Tossing the caber."
How tall is it?	Between 5 and 6 metres.
And what does it weigh?	About 70 kilos.
Wow!	

Facts Check

Pages 8-9: **Possible answers: archery; canoeing; equestrian sport; gymnastics; hockey; karate; mountain biking; orienteering; quoits; X-country running; yachting; (no sport begins with U or Z)**

Page 14: **PUZZLE PIX: (clockwise, starting from top left) f; d; g; h; a; b; c; e
SPORTS FACTS: a. skiing; b. tennis/table tennis; c. the marathon; d. judo; e. cricket; f. polo; g. sumo wrestling; h. skateboarding
SPORTS EQUIPMENT: 1. cycling; 2. table tennis; 3. cricket; 4. underwater swimming; 5. tennis; 6. hockey; 7. skateboarding; 8. ice-skating; 9. baseball; 10. rugby**

Page 16: **FUN CHAT: 2006 Torino; 2008 Beijing; 2010 Vancouver
Winter Games: Torino, Vancouver
Summer Games: Beijing**

GOODBYE!
Well, that's the end of 'Sports'.
Of course, you can continue with your projects. And playing and watching sports. See you in the next Topics title. Bye for now!

Susan Holden